WHALES SET I

HUMPBACK WHALES

Megan M. Gunderson
ABDO Publishing Company

visit us at
www.abdopublishing.com

Published by ABDO Publishing Company, 8000 West 78th Street, Edina, Minnesota 55439. Copyright © 2011 by Abdo Consulting Group, Inc. International copyrights reserved in all countries. No part of this book may be reproduced in any form without written permission from the publisher. The Checkerboard Library™ is a trademark and logo of ABDO Publishing Company.

Printed in the United States of America, North Mankato, Minnesota.
042010
092010

PRINTED ON RECYCLED PAPER

Cover Photo: Peter Arnold
Interior Photos: Alamy pp. 13, 17; Getty Images p. 8; iStockphoto pp. 5, 19;
    Peter Arnold p. 15; Photo Researchers pp. 10, 19, 21; Uko Gorter pp. 7, 9

Editor: Tamara L. Britton
Art Direction & Cover Design: Neil Klinepier

Library of Congress Cataloging-in-Publication Data

Gunderson, Megan M., 1981-
  Humpback whales / Megan M. Gunderson.
      p. cm. -- (Whales)
  Includes index.
  ISBN 978-1-61613-449-5
  1. Humpback whale--Juvenile literature. I. Title.
  QL737.C424G864 2011
  599.5'25--dc22
                                                    2010006286

CONTENTS

HUMPBACKS AND FAMILY 4
SHAPE, SIZE, AND COLOR 6
WHERE THEY LIVE 8
SENSES 10
DEFENSE 12
FOOD 14
BABIES 16
BEHAVIORS 18
HUMPBACK WHALE FACTS 20
GLOSSARY 22
WEB SITES 23
INDEX 24

Humpbacks and Family

Humpback whales are fascinating animals! They sing long songs and make impressive leaps out of the water. These huge **cetaceans** are named for the way they dive. They hunch, or hump, their backs before heading underwater.

Like all mammals, humpback whales are **warm-blooded** and nurse their young. To fill their lungs with air, they surface to breathe. They have a few hairs on their heads and lower jaws. And, there is a layer of **blubber** under the skin.

Humpbacks are **baleen** whales. They are related to blue whales and fin whales. These whales all belong to the family Balaenopteridae.

The markings on a humpback whale's flukes are as unique as human fingerprints. Scientists use these patterns to identify and study individual humpback whales.

Shape, Size, and Color

The humpback whale has a robust body and a large, flattened head. Its dorsal fin can be different heights and shapes. This fin sits on a hump, which shows best when the whale dives.

A large splashguard protects two blowholes. This prevents water from getting into the blowholes when the whale breathes.

This **unique** whale's flippers are the longest of any **cetacean**! The flippers are slender and have knobs along the front edges. Large knobs also appear on the whale's head and lower jaw.

Humpback whales weigh about 66,000 pounds (30,000 kg). Female humpback whales average 43 feet (13 m) in length. Males are a bit shorter. On average, they grow 41 feet (12.5 m) long.

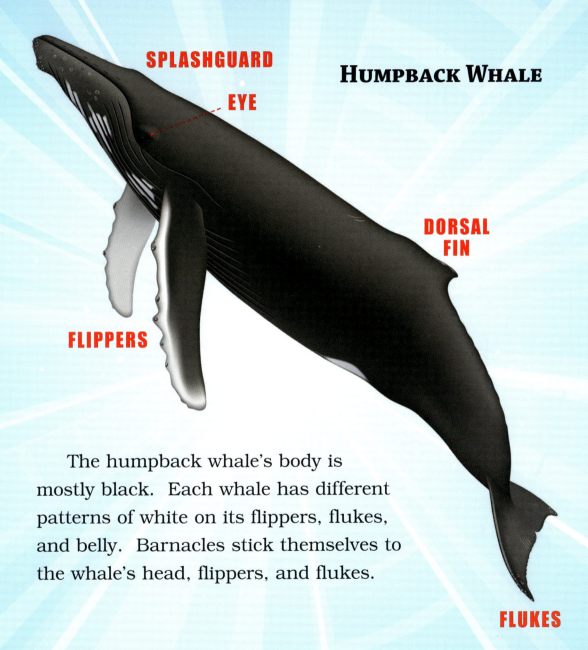

Humpback Whale

SPLASHGUARD
EYE
DORSAL FIN
FLIPPERS
FLUKES

The humpback whale's body is mostly black. Each whale has different patterns of white on its flippers, flukes, and belly. Barnacles stick themselves to the whale's head, flippers, and flukes.

WHERE THEY LIVE

A thick layer of blubber protects humpbacks from cold water.

All of Earth's oceans are home to humpback whales. These whales like coastal areas best. Sometimes, they even swim into harbors and up rivers.

Humpback whales can **migrate** long distances. Some travel up to 9,900 miles (16,000 km) every year! These humpback whales spend summers feeding in cool polar waters. They move to **tropical** and **subtropical** waters in winter to breed.

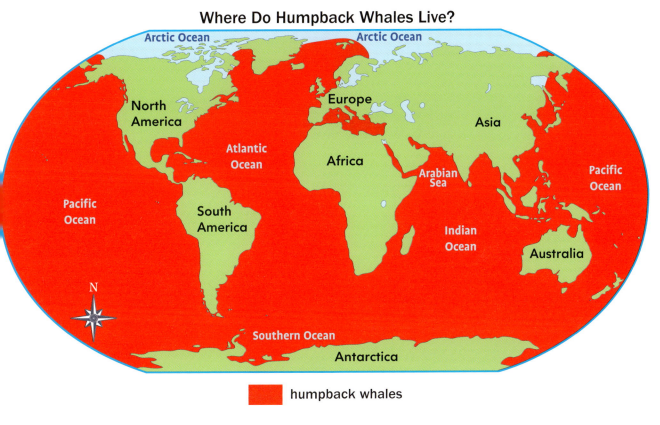

Not all humpback whales **migrate**. A population in the Arabian Sea spends the whole year in **tropical** waters.

Up to 150 humpback whales gather at favorite places to eat. When breeding, groups of three to five are most common. The rest of the time, humpback whales are often seen alone.

Senses

Humpback whales must navigate a huge **habitat**. To survive, they rely on their senses. Humpback whales have a good sense of sight. They can see well underwater. To look around

above water, they bob their heads out. This is called spyhopping.

Touch is another important sense for humpback whales. In fact, mothers touch their young with their flippers to show affection. Scientists are still studying the humpback whale's senses of smell and taste.

Humpback whales make a wide variety of sounds. Listening to one another is important for communication. So, humpback whales also rely on a keen sense of hearing.

Scientists are not sure if humpback whales use echolocation. This process involves sending out sounds and listening for them to echo back. Other whales use echolocation to navigate, find food, and avoid predators.

To spyhop, humpback whales push themselves above water with their flukes.

Defense

Humpback whales have few natural predators. Large sharks may go after ill or injured adults. Killer whales will attack young humpback whales. But this can be challenging! Mother humpback whales become **aggressive** to protect their young from harm.

Humans are the humpback whale's greatest threat. In the 1900s, whalers killed about 90 percent of the world's humpback whales. The whales were easy to catch because they live near shore. And, they are slow swimmers.

Today, humpback whales are protected from hunters. So, most populations are increasing. Yet other human threats remain. Humpback whales sometimes become tangled in fishing nets. And, whale watching boats and other ships accidentally hit and injure them.

Scientists estimate there are more than 60,000 humpback whales worldwide.

Food

Humpback whales do most of their feeding in summer in cool waters. There, they eat up to 3,000 pounds (1,360 kg) of food every day.

Their diet includes **plankton** and tiny **crustaceans** called krill. Humpback whales also eat small schooling fish. Favorites include herring, capelins, and sand lances.

A humpback whale doesn't chomp its food with gigantic teeth. Instead of teeth, it has **baleen** plates. There are 340 plates on each side of the upper jaw.

The humpback whale is a gulp feeder. Its throat expands as it takes in large amounts of food and water. Then, the whale's tongue squeezes the water back out through the baleen. Only the food is left behind for the whale to swallow!

The humpback whale's throat expands thanks to 10 to 36 long pleats on its underside.

Humpback whales have another **unique** way of feeding. Underwater, they blow a circle of bubbles from their blowholes. The bubbles act like nets to capture fish. The humpbacks rush through the bubble nets to gulp down their trapped prey!

Babies

Humpback whales mate in winter. The female is **pregnant** for 11 to 12 months. Then, she gives birth to a single baby. The baby whale is called a calf.

At birth, a humpback calf is 13 to 15 feet (4 to 4.6 m) long. It weighs about 1,500 pounds (680 kg). The calf nurses for 6 to 12 months. During this time, it grows 1.5 feet (.5 m) every month. The calf and its mother stay together for one to two years.

Humpback whales keep growing until they are 15 to 21 years old. They can live to be at least 50. Scientists estimate that some humpbacks have lived up to 77 years!

Female humpback whales have one calf every two to three years.

Behaviors

Humpbacks are more vocal than any other whale. The males are particularly famous for the songs they sing. Their sounds can be heard 20 miles (30 km) away underwater. Some are so loud they can also be heard above water!

Male humpback whales use their songs to attract mates and find group members. Each song lasts 6 to 35 minutes. The whales repeat the song for hours or days at a time. Whales in different areas sing in different dialects. And, the songs change gradually over time.

Humpbacks are also famous for being active above water. They **breach** and **lobtail**. They also slap their flippers on the water's surface. These impressive displays make humpback whales popular with whale watchers.

Flipper slapping (top) and lobtailing (bottom) may be forms of communication.

Humpback Whale Facts

Scientific Name: *Megaptera novaeangliae*

Common Name: Humpback whale

Other Names: Bunch, hump whale, hunchbacked whale

Average Size:
Length - 41 to 43 feet (12.5 to 13 m)
Weight - 66,000 pounds (30,000 kg)

Where They Are Found: In all oceans

The largest humpback whales can grow to 62 feet (19 m) and 90,000 pounds (40,000 kg).

Glossary

aggressive (uh-GREH-sihv) - displaying hostility.

baleen - the tough, hornlike material that hangs from the upper jaw of certain whales. Whales use baleen to filter food.

blubber - the fat of whales and other marine mammals. Blubber protects animals from cold.

breach - to jump or leap up out of water.

cetacean (sih-TAY-shuhn) - a member of the order Cetacea. Mammals such as dolphins, whales, and porpoises are cetaceans.

crustacean (kruhs-TAY-shuhn) - any of a group of animals with a hard shell and jointed legs. Crabs, lobsters, and shrimps are all crustaceans.

habitat - a place where a living thing is naturally found.

lobtail - to slap the water's surface with the flukes.

migrate - to move from one place to another, often to find food.

plankton - small animals and plants that float in a body of water.

pregnant - having one or more babies growing within the body.

subtropical - relating to an area where average temperatures range between 55 and 68 degrees Fahrenheit (13 and 20°C).

tropical - relating to an area with an average temperature above 77 degrees Fahrenheit (25°C) where no freezing occurs.

unique - being the only one of its kind.

warm-blooded - having a body temperature that is not much affected by surrounding air or water.

WEB SITES

To learn more about humpback whales, visit ABDO Publishing Company on the World Wide Web at **www.abdopublishing.com**. Web sites about humpback whales are featured on our Book Links page. These links are routinely monitored and updated to provide the most current information available.

INDEX

A

Arabian Sea 9

B

Balaenopteridae (family) 4
baleen 4, 14
barnacles 7
blowholes 6, 15
blubber 4
breaching 18

C

calves 4, 11, 12, 16
color 7
communication 11

D

defense 10, 12
diving 4, 6
dorsal fin 6

E

echolocation 11

F

flippers 6, 7, 11, 18
flukes 7
food 4, 8, 9, 14, 15, 16

G

groups 9, 18

H

habitat 8, 9, 10, 12, 14
hair 4
head 4, 6, 7, 11
hunting 14, 15

J

jaw 4, 6, 14

L

life span 16
lobtailing 18

M

mammals 4
migration 8, 9

P

population 12

R

reproduction 8, 9, 16, 18

S

senses 10, 11
size 4, 6, 16
skin 4
songs 4, 18
speed 12
splashguard 6
spyhopping 11

T

threats 12, 13
tongue 14